Transnepunian

Ashlin Menard

Presentation by *BookLeaf Publishing*

Web: www.bookleafpub.com

E-mail: info@bookleafpub.com

ISBN: 9789357441124

First edition 2023

For Aurora.

Dark

Hatred spews like lava from my mouth.
These words burn coming up my throat.
My tongue shrivels as they leave it.
The ringing in my ears echoes after hearing
them
And I regret their bitterness.

Your words shoot through my heart,
Like bullets leaving me drained.
Whispers can't hide our anger.
The look in your eyes makes my resolve wither
And sends tears down my cheeks.

Yet even when the words have died,
We slither into our cocoons,
Your heat radiating through the sheets,
I have never felt so cold
And the night has never seemed so dark.

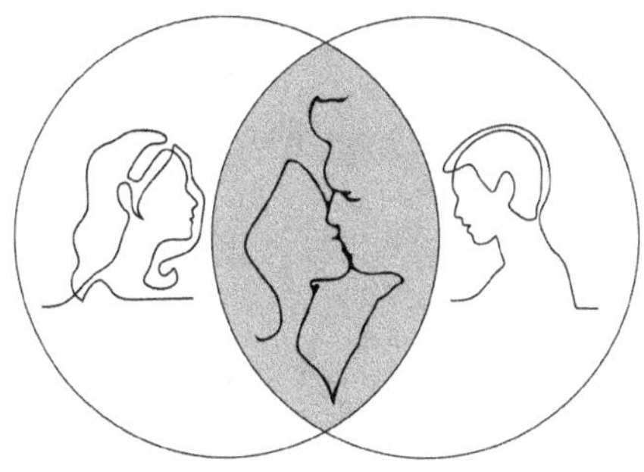

Siren Song

The world down here is dark and bleak.
I suffer in solitude.
No creatures to stir the water,
Just sand and darkness.

Not until unknowing victims float past
Do I leave my lonely depths
And surface in the shallows.
I rise with melodic hymns,
Searching for poor souls to listen.
Luring all attention for miles around,
Notes carrying into every mind,
Taking hold of them and drawing them nearer.

Like children they come to me,
Begging me to take them into my arms.
But only when I bring them to my home,
Empty and hungry,
Do they see the danger
The spell breaks and they flounder in my grasp,
My song drowns in their watery screams.
But still I hold,
Tight and patient,
And soon they perish,
My appetite sufficed – for now.

You have heard the shanties,
And now you have heard my song.
Check your ropes and sail quickly past me
Because you'll never see me coming.

the chase

i know your name.
you know my pain.
we were born into this solitude
that entwines us within each other
to forever circle round
unable to reach across and touch.
forever chasing the other.

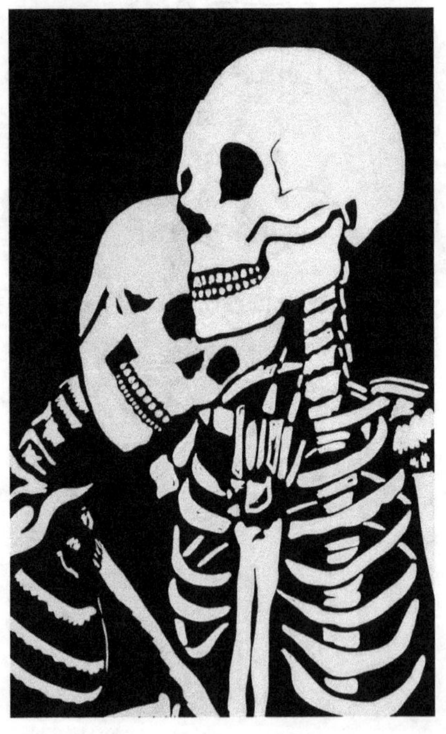

Coffee Milk

Home tastes like coffee milk
Like that first sip in the morning
When it warms you down to your toes.
Like Grammy's spaghetti,
even though now I miss her rice and gravy more.
Or like homemade vanilla ice cream
Where it's a little extra icy.
And like mom's gumbo that
she spends hours cooking.
But especially like that fresh brewed cup,
Because coffee milk tastes like home
And you taste like coffee milk.

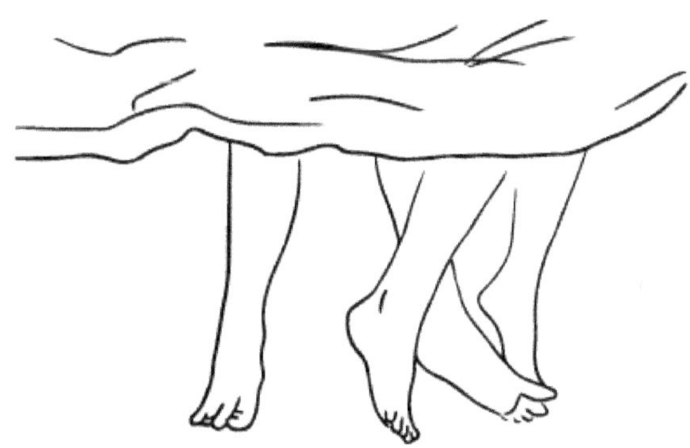

Safety

his hand on my burning skin
my name caressing his tongue
his hair tickling my forehead
my arms reaching across his back
his body blanketing mine
my breath kissing his cheek
his voice in my ear
my hair draped across his shoulders
this is love
this is safety
this is mine.

Poison

The sharpener has to tear off pieces
In order to make a point.
Bodies can destroy themselves
Thinking they are healing.
Trees are cut down to make paper
And paper is used to proclaim
The absurdity of cutting down trees.
Poison only tastes like poison
Once we've swallowed it.

No Reaction

Do you realize what has happened?
You have done exactly
what you said you wouldn't do.
I won't do what you've done to me.
Don't ask me to give you
what you think you need from me.
I know you just want to feel heard
but I can't listen. I don't have the patience
to see you, and I know you just
want a reaction. I'll just stay here
and keep my distance so that
I don't have to witness this.

Transneptunian

If love was measured by distance
Mine could not be contained in this solar system.
It would blow past the moon,
Sling shot around Jupiter,
Wave to Pluto as it passed.
Alpha Centauri would blur as it grew further
away.
It would swim through the Milk Way
And on its way out it would blow a kiss to
Kepler-32.
It would meet the Andromeda Galaxy head on,
And be temporarily blinded by Nembus as it
moves past.
It would pass through the Triangulum Galazy,
Centaurus,
And Bode's Galaxy, weaving its way through
the universe.
It would fly and fly and fly until…
At the edge of the universe the end cannot be
seen,
Forever stretching into the unknown,
Confident in its ability to persevere.
If love was measured by distance,
This would be my love for you.

Drought

When it first peaked out of the ground
I was ecstatic to have something to care for.
You told me to water it every day
Otherwise, I would kill it, a murderer.
Diligently I did, at least once a day.
You even reminded me sometimes,
As if I would forget what you told me to do.
I watered it with my tears
When you drew them out of me.
It appeared healthy and happy
Just as I did on the outside.
I didn't even realize the pressure,
I was under your thumb,
Until at last I was free and could breathe.
It was much later that I realized
I had forgotten the watering.
Without tears to wring into the earth,
It had completely slipped my mind.
Frantically I filled my watering can and
Rushed to hopefully resurrect it.
But it wasn't there anymore.
In its place was a healthy, happy,
And flourishing cactus.
Barbs strong and sharp,
Green and ripe with hope,

Finally growing properly
Without your influence.

the old world

But when they reached the Earth
the world was flat
and the sun was burning.
I was not born to breathe,
I was not worthy to touch,
but I was not powerless to understand
the past had been fruitless.
The old world echoes from the sea,
and the wind spoke in circles to me
of the stories about them,
the old people.

Xander

A beast came down Everest, frozen.
Girls hung irises just knowing love makes no
optimal promises.
Quiet roses silenced the unbearable vices,
While Xander yells

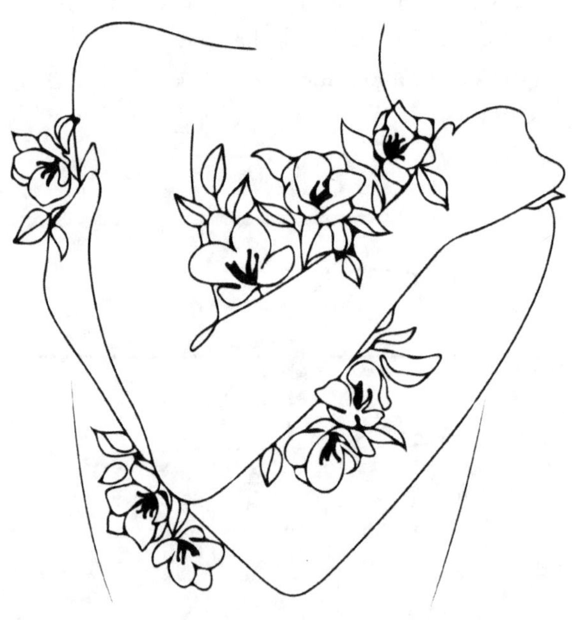

Cul-de-sac

When I was little I
Lived in a cul-de-sac with
A coulee behind my house
An old woman lived in
The blue house and yelled at
Kids in her yard the girl next
Door baby sat us and held me
Back when my mom left
For work the house next
To them was small and had
Two big dogs that were very
Scary across the street was
A friendly neighbor who
Liked to talk with my
Mom and dad after
Hurricanes and when
The eyes would
Pass my sister and I walked
Around the cul-de-sac
Or swam in the pool
Because it doesn't lighting
In a hurricane much and
The ice cream man rarely
Came but the Schwan's truck
Was better because nothing

Could compare to that sweet
Frozen chocolate chip cookie
Dough that was best eaten
Slightly thawed in a mug.

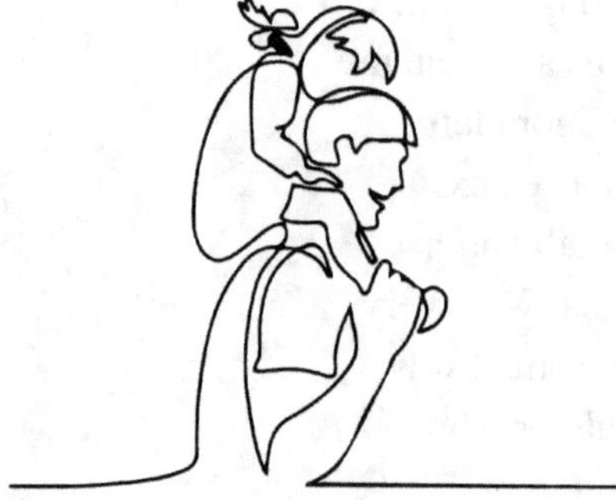

the first sunset

where her hand grazed his soul,
which was bitter and dead,
grew sweet poppies and marigolds
that did not wither in his wasteland.
from his first kiss on her pink cheek
came the first sunset
which blackened the sky
and brought sleep to her land.
the two danced together,
light and dark,
day and night,
life and death
and never tired.
the sun and moon died before they rested
which was only to lie and dream
of the life they wanted together.

When I know

When we lay down in bed
In that room that is always just a little too hot
And cover ourselves with the blanket because
the door doesn't lock,
This is when I know that I love you.

Nyctophobia

I used to be afraid of the dark,
forcing my mother to turn on the hallway light
so as to avoid the creeping shadows.
The way the night moves when light is gone
always caused my heart to race
and my eyes to play foolish tricks on me.
These tricks would lead to sleepless nights
and constant cries for Mama.
Then I found the ease in falling back asleep
when the lights were out.
Drooping eyes less distracted by the possibility
of what could be there.
That is when the dark became my friend,
my most trusted confidant,
the most comfortable blanket
I could wrap myself in to sleep.

brainwashed

who made our ghastly shapes?
whose heart adores me?
how often is nothing defended?
what did a man of blood and sweat say to
convince us all
that we never thought we existed?
when will he speak again?

they named me Dream

They named me Dream
Because I was such a nightmare.
Fragile as a pane of glass
But resilient as cold stone
I refused to die.

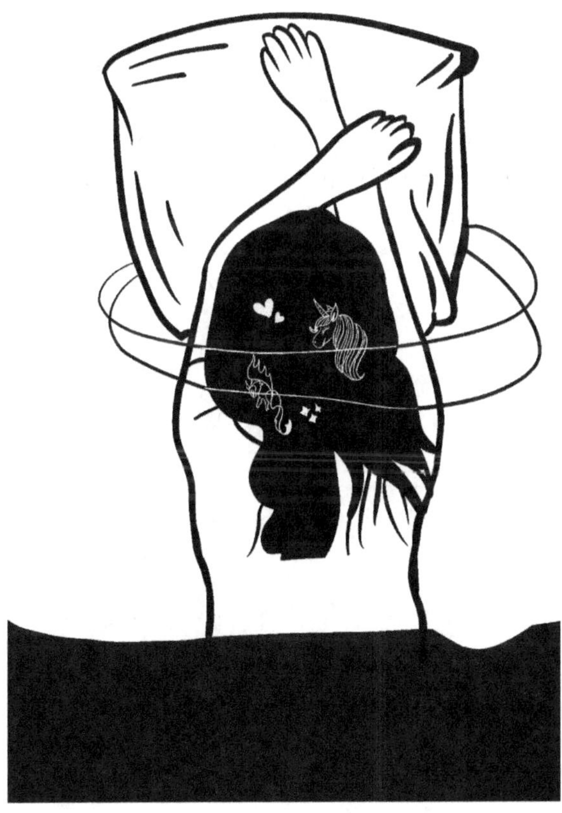

Kissing in the Rain

I always wanted to kiss in the rain
And you always were happy to oblige.
But we are different, our languages mismatched.
My love is a cup, filling up with these watery
kisses.
Yours is a rock, steady and strong,
But still a stone being eroded by the rain pelting
the tops of our heads.
So, with every rainy kiss, my love for you grew,
And your love for me slowly chipped away until
it was no more.

Numbness

I ache to feel what it is to love,
To be loved; to hate and to loathe.
To feel time gripping at me
As it runs away from my grasp.
To feel a splintering in my chest
When my heart decides to break.
To feel my lungs collapse
When my brain is anxious.
But all I feel is numb,
And maybe that hurts too.

Devotion

Devotion cannot describe
Any feelings I have for you.
Violets and roses are nothing
In comparison to how you make me feel.
Drinking sweet nectar,
Like water fresh from a glacier,
Antagonizingly slow, yet delicious
When picked from the
Right vine.
Every hair on my body stands,
Nerves quivering at your touch.
Certainly, you must know when
Every move you make does.
Fiercely, my heart adores you,
Longingly, my hands reach for you.
Only you can cause this burning which
Runs through me like electricity.
Even through tragedy
Nothing can dampen this fire
That rages inside my heart.
Intimate moments,
Nothings in my ear,
Old lovers in past lives,
My nighttime darling.
Evergreen, growing stronger,

Never graying, making goodbyes harder.
Affection in its truest form,
Rendering me useless without you.
Devotion, it is not enough to say
I love you.

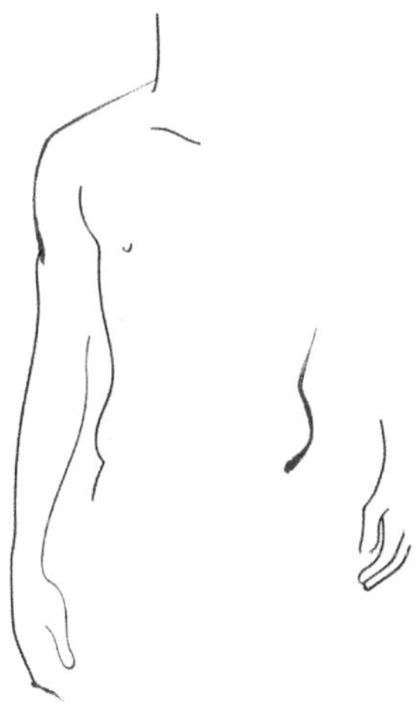

Looking for a poem

I am looking for a poem.
Some say it's in the heart,
Some say it's in the fingers.
Some even say it's in the pen.
But really, it's been gone
Far too long for me to write it.
It flew away when I denied it
And now it won't return.

I have to find it.